Crafts from Salt Dough

by Audrey Gessat

Translated by Cheryl L. Smith

Reading Consultant:
Dr. Robert Miller
Professor of Special Education
Minnesota State University, Mankato

Bridgestone Books
an imprint of Capstone Press
Mankato, Minnesota

Table of Contents

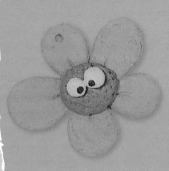

words to Know

acrylic paint (uh-KRIL-ik PAYNT)—a type of paint made from chemicals

consistency (kuhn-SIS-tuhn-see)—the degree of firmness or thickness a mixture has; dough must be at the right consistency for crafts.

ingredient (in-GREE-dee-uhnt)—an item that something is made from; ingredients usually are part of a recipe.

knead (NEED)—to press, fold, and stretch dough to make it smooth

proportion (pruh-POR-shuhn)—the relationship of two or more sizes or amounts to each other

super glue (SOO-pur GLOO)—a very strong glue often used to repair broken objects; only adults should use super glue.

varnish (VAR-nish)—a thick liquid used to protect objects; varnish dries clear.

Originally published as *Pâte à Sel*, © 1999 Editions Milan

Bridgestone Books are published by Capstone Press
151 Good Counsel Drive, P.O. Box 669, Mankato, Minnesota 56002
http://www.capstone-press.com

Library of Congress Cataloging-in-Publication Data
Gessat, Audrey.
  [Pâte à sel. English]
  Crafts from salt dough/by Audrey Gessat.
  p. cm.—(Step by step)
  Includes index.
  Summary: Describes how to make salt dough and provides detailed instructions with photographs for making twelve crafts.
  ISBN 0-7368-1475-2 (hardcover)
  1. Bread dough craft—Juvenile literature. [1. Bread dough craft. 2. Handicraft.] I. Title. II. Step by step (Mankato, Minn.)
TT880 .G4713 2003
745.5—dc21   2002005018

1 2 3 4 5 6 07 06 05 04 03 02

Editor:
Rebecca Glaser

Photographs:
Milan/Dominique Chauvet;
Capstone Press/Gary Sundermeyer

Graphic Design:
Sarbacane

Design Production:
Steve Christensen

Some Secrets about Salt Dough

There are many salt dough recipes. Each person finds his or her own tricks and proportion of ingredients. After a few tries, write down your favorite recipe. Here is the one used to make the crafts in this book.

Ingredients:
- ¾ cup (175 mL) flour
- ⅔ cup (150 mL) salt
- ¾ cup (175 mL) cornstarch
- ⅔ cup (150 mL) water

1 Mix the flour, salt, and cornstarch in a salad bowl. The cornstarch gives the dough a better consistency. If you do not have cornstarch, you can add more flour.

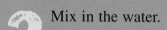
Mix in the water.

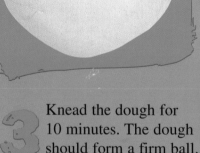
3 Knead the dough for 10 minutes. The dough should form a firm ball.

4

Hints and Tricks

→ To see if your dough has the right consistency, put a little of it on the table. If it spreads out, add a little flour. If it crumbles, add water 1 tablespoon (15 mL) at a time.

→ If you have leftover dough, you can store it in the refrigerator in a plastic bag or in a covered plastic dish.

cooking

It is not necessary to cook your crafts. You can let them air dry, but it will take longer. If you cook them, they will be stronger. Cooking the dough can be tricky. For best results, let your crafts dry for a day before putting them in the oven.

1. Preheat oven to 200°F (93°C).
2. Place your objects on a cookie sheet or aluminum pie pan.
3. Ask an adult to put them in the oven for you.
4. Take your dough crafts out of the oven after three hours. Let them cool. Tap the object with your fingernail to make sure it is done. If the sound is light, the craft is cooked. If the sound is heavy, cook it a little longer.

caution

- Never use the oven by yourself.
- Ask an adult to put your objects in the oven and take them out.
- Do not touch your crafts until you are sure they are cool.
- Be careful not to touch the aluminum pie pan or the cookie sheet while they are hot. You could burn yourself.

Materials

salad bowl

measuring cup

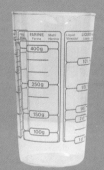

rolling pin

wooden spatula

butter knife

aluminum pie pan or cookie sheet

aluminum foil

paint

dish of water

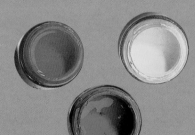

paintbrush

tacky glue

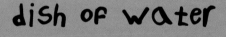

6

Be careful   Super glue must be used by an adult.

Basic Shapes

balls

pancakes

sausages

Friendly Advice

→ To make these crafts, start with simple shapes like balls, sausages, and pancakes. Then cut or shape them according to the directions.

→ Work on a cookie sheet or pie pan so you can put your objects in the oven without tearing them.

→ As you work, your dough may dry out. Dip your fingertips in water and then knead the dough to make it the right consistency again.

→ Thick dough takes a long time to cook. To make a large shape, first make an aluminum foil ball. Then cover it with dough. The dough should not be thicker than ⅜ inch (1 centimeter).

→ To connect two pieces of dough, wet the area of contact with a paintbrush dipped in water. Use the wet paintbrush to smooth the area where the pieces meet.

→ When the dough is cooked or dry, you can paint it with acrylic paint.

→ You can varnish your crafts to protect them and give them a shiny appearance. Ask an adult to help you with the varnish.

→ If an object breaks, ask an adult to glue it back together with super glue.

7

Flower Necklace

You Will Need:

- **Rolling pin**
- **Wooden spatula**
- **Toothpick**
- **Paint**
- **Paintbrush**
- **Yarn or string**

 Make a ball of dough. Flatten it with a rolling pin to make a pancake.

 Cut out a flower with a wooden spatula.

3 Poke a hole in the top petal with a toothpick.

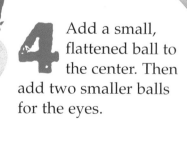 **4** Add a small, flattened ball to the center. Then add two smaller balls for the eyes.

 **5** When the flower is cooked, paint it as you wish. String the flower on the yarn to make a necklace.

8

Use the toothpick to poke small holes in the center of the flower before you cook it. The holes make it look like a real flower. Real flowers have many small parts in their centers that hold pollen. Insects spread these tiny grains from flower to flower so the flowers can make new seeds.

airplane clothespin

1 Form a sausage of dough about the size of a clothespin. Make it a little thinner at one end. Cut out wings and tail pieces from a pancake of dough.

2 Assemble the pieces with a wet paintbrush.

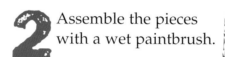

3 When the plane has cooked, paint it. You can also paint the clothespin.

4 When the paint has dried, glue the airplane to the clothespin with strong glue.

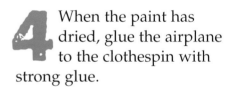

10

William and Orville Wright flew the first successful airplane in 1903. The first flight lasted only 12 seconds.

11

Lamb Pin

3 Stick the strands to the body and the top of the head with a wet paintbrush.

1 Form two flattened ovals, one for the body and one for the head. Put them together and add ears. Stick in four toothpicks for the legs. Add a small piece of dough for the tail.

2 To make the wool, press some dough through a strainer and carefully remove the strands.

4 When your craft is cooked, paint the head and the legs black. Paint eyes and nostrils.

5 Ask an adult to attach the lamb to a pin back with super glue.

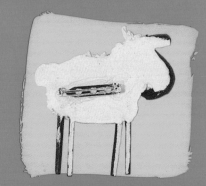

Suffolk is a type of sheep with a black head and face, black legs, and white wool. This type came from Suffolk County in England.

zebra Magnet

2 Press one magnet into the back of the head and two into the back of the body.

1 Cut out the body and the head from a dough pancake. Make ears and feet. Attach the ears to the head.

4 Attach the legs and the head by gluing the yarn to the body. Add more yarn for the tail.

3 When the parts are cooked, paint them. Glue a strand of yarn to each foot and to the head.

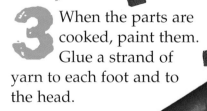

14

Both zebras and giraffes have one-of-a-kind patterns on their fur. No two zebras or two giraffes have the same fur patterns. They are as different as human fingerprints.

15

Dominoes

1 Make a dough ball and flatten it with a rolling pin to form a pancake.

2 Cut rectangles out of the dough. Trace a line in the middle of each rectangle with the wooden spatula.

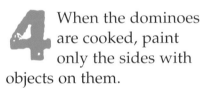

3 With a knife, cut out two matching objects from thin dough. Wet the objects with the paintbrush. Stick one object to a dough rectangle. Stick the matching object to another rectangle. Make 20 dominoes to have enough for a game.

4 When the dominoes are cooked, paint only the sides with objects on them.

16

Most dominoes have certain numbers of dots on each end. The dots are called "pips."

Rules:

Two or more people can play dominoes.

1. Place all the dominoes face down on a table.
2. Each player picks 5 dominoes.
3. Choose one player to start. The first player plays one domino.
4. The next player must play a domino with a side that matches the first domino. If a player cannot match a domino on the table, he or she must draw from the pile.
5. Players take turns matching dominoes until one person plays all of his or her dominoes. This person wins.

17

clown pencil

You Will Need:

- **Pencil**
- **Oven-safe glass jar**
- **Paint**
- **Paintbrush**

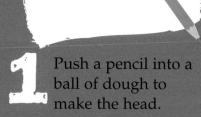

1 Push a pencil into a ball of dough to make the head.

2 Add a pointed hat, a ball for the nose, and two tiny pancakes for the ears.

3 Place your pencil in an oven-safe jar to cook the dough. Make sure the jar can stand up in the oven.

4 When the clown head is cooked, you can paint it.

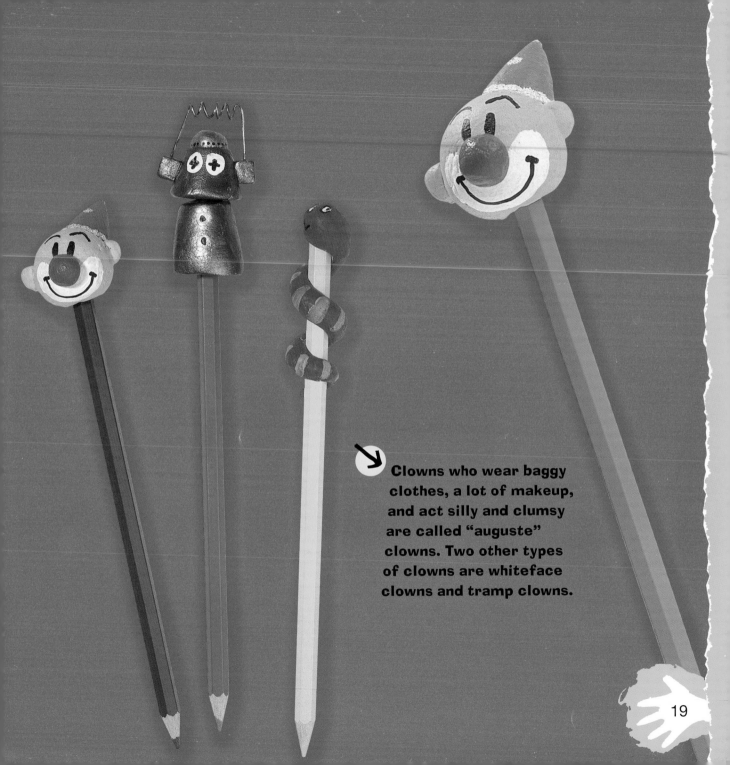

Clowns who wear baggy clothes, a lot of makeup, and act silly and clumsy are called "auguste" clowns. Two other types of clowns are whiteface clowns and tramp clowns.

19

Porcupine Pencil Holder

You Will Need:
- **Aluminum foil**
- **Round pencil**
- **Paint**
- **Paintbrush**

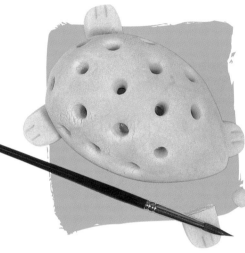

3 Attach a nose and legs by wetting the dough with a paintbrush.

1 Form a large pear shape with the aluminum foil. Do not pack the foil too tightly. Flatten it a little on one side. Cover the foil with dough.

2 With a round pencil, gently poke holes into the dough as far as the foil.

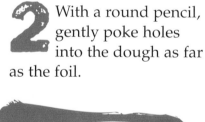

4 When the craft is cooked, use your pencil to push in the foil. Paint your pencil holder.

20

A porcupine's quills stick out only when it is scared. A porcupine defends itself from another animal by hitting it with its quilled tail. The quills stick in the animal. New quills grow to replace the ones the porcupine lost.

21

Snail Picture Holder

You Will Need:
- Aluminum foil
- Butter knife
- Toothpicks

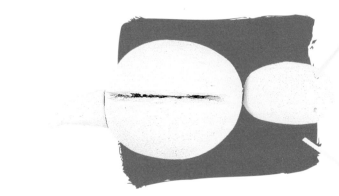

1 Make a ball with the foil. Do not pack it tightly. Make a slit in the foil with the butter knife. Cover the foil with dough. Reopen the slit with the butter knife.

3 Assemble the head and the shell. Add the tail by using a wet paintbrush. Stick four toothpicks for the feelers in the head.

2 Make the head by covering a second ball of foil with dough.

4 When your snail is cooked, paint it.

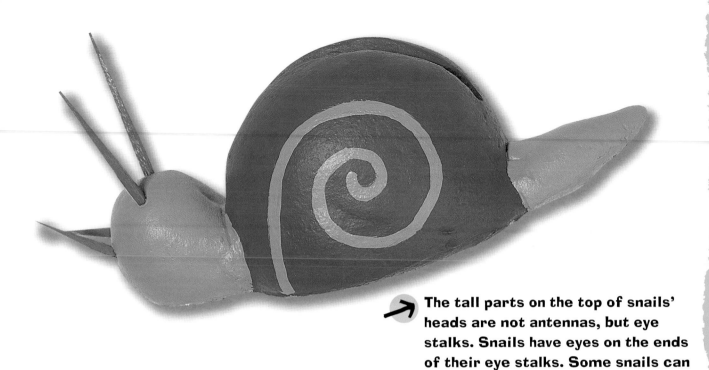

The tall parts on the top of snails' heads are not antennas, but eye stalks. Snails have eyes on the ends of their eye stalks. Some snails can pull their eye stalks into their head.

23

Turtle Treasure Holder

You Will Need:
- **Aluminum foil**
- **Paintbrush**
- **Water**
- **Paint**

1 For the body, form a large ball with crumpled foil. Do not pack it too tightly. Flatten the ball on one side. Hollow out the other side with your fingers to form a nest.

2 Form a little ball of foil for the head. Cover the head and the body with dough.

3 Assemble the body and the head. Cut out the feet and the tail from a pancake of dough. Stick them to the shell with a little water.

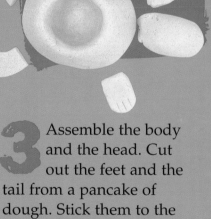

4 When the turtle is cooked, paint it.

24

Sea turtles lay their eggs on land. They bury the eggs to protect them from other animals who might eat them.

25

Hanging Bee

You Will Need:
- **Paintbrush**
- **Toothpicks**
- **Wire**
- **Paint**
- **Paper**
- **Scissors**
- **Tacky glue**
- **Nylon string**

2 Break a toothpick in two and gently put one half into the front of the head. Poke two tiny holes on the top of the head with a toothpick.

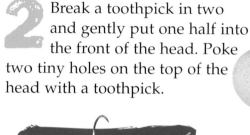

1 Make a round ball for the head and an oval ball for the body. Assemble them with a wet paintbrush.

3 Ask an adult to help you with the wire. Stick a small wire loop into the back of the bee. After the craft is cooked, glue the wire antennas into the tiny holes on the head. Paint the bee.

4 Cut out wings from paper.

5 When the paint is dry, glue the wings to the back of the bee. Then tie a nylon string to the loop on the back.

26

Bees drink a sweet liquid called nectar from flowers. They use a long, tubelike body part to sip the nectar.

27

candleholder

3 Prepare small decorative shapes such as balls, coils, flowers, or animals. Stick them to the pancake with a little water.

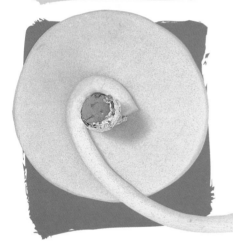

2 Add a ball to make the head of the snake.

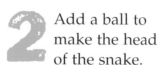

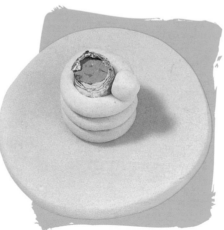

1 Make a large dough pancake. Cover the cork with foil and put it in the center of the pancake. Make a large dough sausage. Roll the dough sausage around the cork to make a snake.

4 When your candleholder is cooked, remove the cork. Paint your craft.

Long ago, Romans made candles from tallow, or melted fat from cattle or sheep.

Be careful! An adult must light the candle.

29

Doorknob Hanger

You Will Need:
- Two glasses of different sizes (both wider than a doorknob)
- Thick wire
- Pipe cleaner (chenille stem)
- Tacky glue

1 Make a dough pancake. Cut out a circle with the larger glass. Use the smaller glass to cut out a circle in the center.

2 Add a ball of dough for the head. Ask an adult to help you with the wire. Add wire legs and arms. Place the body on top of the wire. Add dough hands and feet. Form the letters of your name with little sausages or cut them out of a thin pancake. Place them on the ring in the right order.

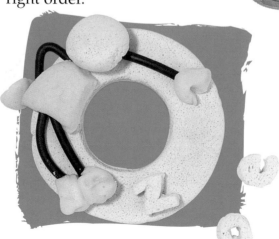

3 When your project is cooked, paint it. When the paint is dry, glue on the pipe cleaner to look like hair. Hang the craft on your doorknob.

Pipe cleaners really are used to clean tobacco pipes. Many people use colored pipe cleaners for crafts. Some pipe cleaners are made from a type of yarn called chenille. They are called "chenille stems."

index

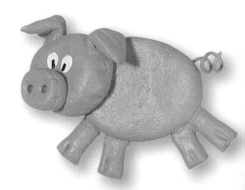